# HOW TO
# DEAL WITH
# WHITE PEOPLE

D1602949

## By

## David Goldberg

First Edition

ISBN: 978-0-615-32800-3

www.dealwithwhites.com

FOR L.L.C. IN C.C.

# HOW TO
# DEAL WITH
# WHITE PEOPLE

# <u>CONTENTS</u>

**CHAPTER ONE**
*A Brief History of White People   9*

**CHAPTER TWO**
*Understanding White People   17*

**CHAPTER THREE**
*Communicating With White People   27*

**CHAPTER FOUR**
*White People in the Workplace   33*

**CHAPTER FIVE**
*Police   39*

**CHAPTER SIX**
*White People in Entertainment   47*

**CHAPTER SEVEN**
*White and Non-White Gender Relations   59*

**CHAPTER EIGHT**
*The Mask   65*

**CHAPTER NINE**
*The Trap   71*

**CHAPTER TEN**
*"I Wish I Were White" People   83*

**CHAPTER ELEVEN**
*Pre-Response to Critics   91*

**CHAPTER TWELVE**
*"Cool" White People   97*

# CHAPTER ONE
## A BRIEF HISTORY OF WHITE PEOPLE

Caucasians come from damp and cold Europe.

Cold means you stay indoors, avoiding sunlight. Little sunlight means lack of vitamin A, which affects bone growth and mood.

Imagine living in these conditions over thousands of years. Would one be social? Or pleasant and accepting of others?

Now consider The Black Plague arriving from the east.

The Plague forced white people from their homes. Sent them west in search of more suitable lands.

But the only problem is Western Europe ends in water.

The Atlantic Ocean.

Thus began the most pivotal event in world history: The European Expansion.

In search of resources and land, White people sailed all over the world.

They went to:

Asia,

Africa,

Australia,

Alaska,

South America,

North America,

India,

Everywhere.

And the people of these new lands or "new worlds" welcomed them oblivious to the grave mistake that they were making.

White people arrived. They claimed the lands. And the resources. They told the people of these lands, "If you're not white, you're not right."

How else are the Dutch at the bottom of the African continent claiming to be Africans? If nothing's wrong with that, then where is the African country in Amsterdam or Belgium?

## "IDENTIFYING WHITES BY NAME"

There are all types of whites spread throughout the globe. The ethnicities can vary.

To distinguish, let's examine a few last names.

Some say if the surname ends in a vowel then that's Italian. "Maggiano", "Romano", etc. Some of the things Italians are known for are fine clothing, automobiles, and food.

To identify Irish, look for last names with an "MC" or an "O", as in McCormick or O'Brien. There are several others. You will find that many police and firemen are Irish. Geographically, Ireland is not strategically positioned to benefit from the maritime exploits of its neighboring countries. Therefore, some Irish endure a little more hardships than other whites.

Also, if and when a non-white encounters an Irish police officer, this frustration will be exacted upon that person of color.

To help you place Jewish people by name, look for names that have the "ie" in them such as Weiss, Klein, Stein, or Lieb. You can also take note of names with "berg" or "man" at the end, like "Brachman", "Gorman", "Gold", or "Silver".

Jewish people are very important to understanding the

current state of the world. It is in your absolute best interest to learn as much as you can about them, from surname variations to the influence they wield.

Money, banking, entertainment, information? These are all industries that are controlled and run by Jewish people.

You can get nothing done in this world without being Jewish-approved. Take it from a Jewish kid.

There are many other ethnicities to help you identify whites by surname: Polish, Russian, Norwegian, Armenian, etc. This is just an overview. It benefits you to know exactly what type of white person you are dealing with and the ethnicity that they claim.

Always remember however, that no matter which way you slice it, they are all still white.

## **"WHITE 'SUPREMACY' "**

Whites have always maintained an air of superiority. But here is an actual fact: the phenotypes, white skin, blonde hair and blue eyes are the weakest. The recessive.

Recessive means opposite of dominant, as in weak. Weak is not superior. The white gene is the weakest. Recessive.

Do note, however, that it is very important that throughout time, white people have and must continue to project an image of superiority in order to mislead non-whites.

This is done by repetition through media saturation. The white image must be force-fed over and over to drive a false sense of supremacy home because by nature whites are not superior.

So, when Caucasians call you a nigger, a spic, a chink, a wetback, a beaner, you call them a recessive. They know exactly what the term means.

Or for added amusement, reverse the insult and call them the nigger, for they were the ones that taught the word and behavior in the first place.

## "A COMMON HOSTILITY"

Rule #1: Whites will steal your land and pretend they are entitled to it.

People of color the world over are all in the same predicament. They have all been exploited by one singular group: White people.

Globally, from Australia to Alaska and everywhere in between, people of color are on the receiving end of hostility from whites.

It's a uniform constant.

For instance, before White people came to India, Africa, and Brazil, there was no AIDS.

White people came.

AIDS came.

End of story.

Or take another example. In the years 1884-85, white men from Europe banded together and decided how to carve up and divide Africa amongst themselves without any input from a soul in Africa.

This was called The Berlin Convention.

To put this in proper perspective, imagine you are in your home relaxing. But unbeknownst to you, another group of men are deciding how to divide up your home and property without so much as even discussing it with you.

Whites have done this to people of color on their home continents all over the world.

This vital part of white people's history is instrumental in understanding race relations between Caucasians and non-whites.

To add further insult to the injury, you will notice that whites refer to people of color as "minorities". When in actuality, it is and always has been them that are the true minorities. There are more non-white, people of color on this planet than Caucasians.

White people are the only minorities. Feel free to refer to them as such.

## "DWELLING IN THE PAST"

Perhaps you've heard this before. "Oh, what's done is done", "You people need to just let it go", "Gosh! You're dwelling in the past", or "Let's move forward".

Discussing history is always a progressive step in a forward direction.

Since history is the best metric for measuring future trends, then the survival of people of color will depend upon their reevaluation of their interactions with whites.

History is known to naturally repeat itself. It's imperative that non-whites take a long, hard look at the history of white folk.

Everyone considers history. Banks. Jobs. Schools.

Now, suddenly, people of color should disregard the history of whites? Perhaps not.

The only edge whites have allowing them to dominate non-whites in a world where Caucasians are the true minorities is information.

As people of color become more informed and begin to understand the nature and the history of whites, the exploitation of people of color will grind to a halt and the playing field will begin to even out.

# CHAPTER TWO
## UNDERSTANDING WHITE PEOPLE

There is a delicate balance that you'll maintain in dealing with whites when your words and mannerisms reflect a solid education and awareness of the current real state of race relations.

You'll also exude a calm confidence when you can predict the actions of whites based on the knowledge of their past.

One of the best ways to deal with white people is to have a thorough working knowledge of their habits and motivations.

True, whites did quite a number on people of color. This must be acknowledged, but it's equally important that a few typical misconceptions regarding racism are cleared up.

First off, no energy should be spent trying to reform that which despises you.

NEVER EVER.

Whites don't despise you because you're dark.

They don't despise you because your neighborhood is bad, or because you "can't read good".

They don't discriminate against you because your car isn't registered and you don't have a license.

They don't despise you because you don't own any real estate, but you bought some new sneakers.

They don't hate you because you have thick hair or a wide nose or because you're not educated or because you use double negatives.

They hate you...Just because.

Just because you're not white. It's that simple.

Waste not energy on those who despise you, whether through attempts at changing them or yourselves.

Your accomplishments do not alter their view of you.

None of these reasons contributed to their hatred from the onset.

Understand that there have to be LAWS enacted to force Caucasians to respect people that are non-white.

Think about that.

A law.

This suggests that respect for people of color does not occur naturally in whites.

It's pointless to waste energy being upset with them for their nature. Accept white people for what they have shown you they are and not what you want them to be.

## "REJECTION OF DIFFERENCE"

It is only fair to consider how thousands of years of living in harsh conditions could affect Caucasians thus contributing to an incessant fear of everything.

This fear is often manifested as revulsion when they reject anyone different from themselves.

Whites are difference intolerant. In other words, difference in any form is not, has not, and will not be accepted by them.

## "WE BUILT THIS COUNTRY"

Imagine you own a company called Unitron Corp.

You have a two-hundred floor skyscraper downtown with your microchips in every cell phone. You are a gazillionaire. In fact, the people on printed money actually look like you and are not white.

Are the janitors and mailroom clerks that work in your skyscraper entitled to the same stock options as you and your shareholders?

*You* came up with the plan. *They* are just the grunts.

This is the whites' perspective on people of color who have either toiled in slavery or slave-like labor.

You are entitled to nothing. You are more than expendable. You are just cogs in their grand scheme.

Even poor whites who are not connected to this grand scheme--whites who may come from poor families will always treat you like you are dirt and they are of royal blood.

This is because you are as your people are. The image of whites is communicated as success and material wealth. That is why so many rappers appear foolish boasting their money and riches when people the world over with their skin complexions are poor. The richest people of color will always be mistreated by whites because in white people's mind only people with white skin run the world.

## "GETTING FAMILIAR"

Understanding whites requires familiarization through general observations. Let's examine a few. Over time you will notice more.

Whites will push you as far as possible until you stop them. They will not stop themselves. It's up to you to create boundaries early and often.

For instance, whites will discover sudden surges of courage when accompanied by a medium to large-sized dog. Whereas, they would not so much as make eye contact with a person of color when alone, accompanied by a dog they will be bold and even more offensive.

To counter this, always level your attention with the white person that owns the dog. Do not smile or laugh. Don't focus on the dog. Avoid interacting with the dog owner until they are without canine.

Never let white people stand behind you. No matter what they say, whites are constantly examining, watching, and scrutinizing you. As soon as you sense someone white standing behind you, turn around immediately and look them in the eyes. They will excuse themselves and give you your space. Standing behind you affords them the opportunity to tip confrontational odds to their favor.

Caucasians can only operate with an unfair advantage.

Like white person plus a dog, or

White person plus a position of power, or

White person plus standing behind you, or

White person plus sitting high on a horse or pickup truck, or

White person plus twelve to fifteen of his cohorts setting a home on fire in the dead of the night while women and children sleep.

And, make no mistake, Caucasians will find zero shame in claiming a victory from these uneven odds.

## "DISCONNECTED"

The drum is the life-force of people of color.

All non-white people have drums in their music. The Aborigines, Indonesians, Asians, East Indians, Africans, North, South and African Americans. They all need music that they can feel. That's why the bass drum is central.

White people hate drums or any kind of bass because you can feel bass. And white people don't like to feel anything. So, they de-emphasize the drums or bass in their music. Only leaving you with what you can hear. Not what you can feel.

With strings – guitars, violins - you can hear those, but you can't feel them. Caucasians don't want experiences that can be felt. For whites, experiences that evoke small, disconnected responses are best.

To further understand whites, use the drum example in addition to the callousness displayed during the European expansion to note how they are not connected to the rest of the people on the planet. Whites not only display a total disregard for people of color, but their disdain also applies to all other life and ecological systems on the planet, as well, from wildlife to oceans to rainforests and everything in between.

There has never been a time when white people have gotten along fine with people of color, or anything else on the planet. Never. They have always been disconnected.

This natural disconnection forces whites to emphasize a strong focus on self-created external objects and systems. Like money, cars, gadgets, iPhones, iPods, watches, GPS navigation systems, laptops…everything that is unnatural and synthetic or outside of one's self.

This is why most interactions with whites revolve around the same thing: "How can I make you feel as uncomfortable, afraid, and disconnected as I am?" White people are always paranoid and on edge, and they will try their hardest to make you experience the same levels of anxiety that they feel.

One of the biggest solutions to dealing with whites is to know them. Know them inside and out. Then you can predict their actions.

In the meantime, however, you are better suited to be proactive with white people. So, for best results, mistreat them first before they have a chance to mistreat you.

## "THE GREAT RACE DEBATE"

No such thing.

There is no great race debate.

Whites will never discuss race honestly, openly, and fairly.

In fact, there would not even be such a thing as "race" if it were not for whites. They have made the differences in cultures a competition. They don't call it a "race" for nothing.

Whites will only include non-whites when it's time to cast blame, or if aliens come to visit in a sci-fi story. Suddenly, "humans" or "man" are poisoning the Earth together. Or "all of us" are destroying the planet.

But when it's time to go amass some wealth, only the white people are allowed to go.

Or when a person of color wanted to get a job, white people pretended not to see them.

Or if a Latina woman wanted to have a baby in a white hospital, they acted like she was dirty.

But when it's time to cast blame and discuss the ills of the world, now it's "us".

As far as white people are concerned, it never has been an "us".

Consider this: everyone that ever tried to help people of color or even fought in great racial debates has been killed.

Not just silenced or paid off but killed.

Think about that.

That sends a strong message to any non-white who might be thinking along the lines of "people of color, let's all come together. Let's unite".

Just knowing that they killed every one of the non-white leaders that stood up for equal rights is enough to terrorize non-whites into conformity.

But it's important to understand one truth: whites are more afraid of you than you should ever be of them.

So, go on and unite.

Because everything about whites is not only disconnected from non-whites, it's nearly opposite of the rest of the world. Even down to the way you must communicate with them.

# CHAPTER THREE
## COMMUNICATING WITH WHITE PEOPLE

If you decode or translate everything that Caucasians say and re-filter it through a racist bigot's standpoint then you will have a better understanding of the true meanings of their words and intentions.

With the exception of rhythm, dance, and drums, whites understand all methods of communication whether spoken or non-verbal.

### "JUNGLE LAW"

White people pretend to think that people of color are "primitive natives" although it has always been whites that have exhibited the true animalistic behavior. So, if Caucasians interact with people of color as if they are animals, then the primary forms of non-verbal communication with white people should be rooted in savagery. For this is the language they understand.

Bearing this in mind, occasionally, you may have to yell at white people. You are going to have to stare them down so that they respect your space. Maybe even bump into them when passing on the street.

Never make the mistake of talking to whites about racism.

They know everything regarding the subject forward and backward.

The laws of self preservation don't allow them to be honest in race-related conversations anyway. It's difficult for them to have a discussion that sheds light on the crimes of their race. They may try to over-intellectualize it or just flat out lie. Save yourself the hassle.

They only feign ignorance to pick your brain, using your opinions as amusement to entertain themselves. Treating you like a kid recounting a story that they already know the ending to.

And just as in the wild, never say "thank you" to white people and never apologize. It will only be exploited as a sign of weakness or being passive.

If you feel the urge to say "thanks", just say "cool".

Jungle law serves to avoid unnecessary aggravation until you are faced with no other choice but to actually speak with whites.

## "WE NEED TO TALK"

Now since a face-to-face conversation is more real, more human, more connecting, whites will try their best to avoid these interactions. Only to replace them with letters, emails, text messages, and maybe a phone call.

When you do find yourself in conversation with whites, you are often forced to speak to them in an almost robotic, inhuman manner. The reason you can't speak to white people in your natural tone is because they think it's their job to constantly correct you, scold you, and straighten you out.

And their favorite thing to correct is your English. They'll always treat you like even you don't know what you're saying. So, the right way to talk to them is to raise your voice and almost yell at them when speaking...first. When you speak to them naturally, even though they hear you, they'll pretend not to understand you.

All things considered, the single most effective method of speaking with whites, however, is to broaden your vocabulary.

How?

Read plenty of fiction that does not get marketed to your ethnic group. In other words, blaze through the novels whites read. Just a few here and there.

A broad vocabulary is essential for speaking with white people. It allows you to understand the language they speak, even if you choose not to speak it yourself on a regular day to day basis.

When you speak to white people in an articulate, intelligent manner, sometimes they'll be shocked because they expect you to speak foolishly or to fulfill a stereotype that they created.

In verbal exchanges with Caucasians, you will note that they will always answer your questions with a question. That's how you flip the control of a conversation. It's a way of establishing false dominance, a way of re-shifting subservience and control, which are two things paramount to white people.

There are many reasons white people will ask you to repeat yourself.

White people feel that when speaking to someone of color, they should be addressed through some sort of medium, as if a person of color does not have the right to speak to them directly. So, with irritation, they will ask you to repeat yourself.

White people would like to be addressed in a submissive tone when being spoken to by non-whites. So, asking you to repeat yourself is giving you a second chance. A chance to be submissive.

In conversation, there are different ways to deal with white people when they ask you to repeat yourself unnecessarily.

There is the proactive approach. Raise your voice a notch or two when speaking, locking your eyes with theirs in a cold, death stare. This might cause some whites to cry at first. But they won't have the chance to ask you to repeat yourself.

There is the reactive approach. You can ignore them when they ask you to repeat yourself and they will magically repeat your words.

And, of course, the offensive approach. In place of repeating yourself you mutter something like "toubob" or "gwai-loh" a few notches below your speaking voice and whites will gasp.

Know that white people will use many other tactics to show disrespect during a conversation. For instance, they will talk without looking at you. Ignore them with this or delay your response until they acknowledge you. They hate it if you have or assume that you have equal leverage with them in a conversation.

Whites have no problem approaching you and assuming their "authoritative" tone. When this occurs, for amusement, in your clearest speaking voice, respond with, "I don't speak English."

The irony and humor of that statement should keep your mood upbeat until you are forced into your next encounter with a white person.

# CHAPTER FOUR
## WHITE PEOPLE IN THE WORKPLACE

Understand this.

Two things.

Number One: The office is white people's turf.

Number Two: If you are not white, every day at the office is your first day on the job. Doesn't matter if you've been there for thirty years. It's still your first day. And you will be treated as such. With the minimal respect given to someone who "must be new".

Now since the office is white people's turf, then on this turf, they'll feel courageous. Brazen. Daring. More comfy.

And they're most comfortable behind a desk…and in front of a computer…with a cup a coffee. Isolated and disconnected from other life.

People of color only function in this hostile environment out of pure necessity.

White people assume that non-whites' apprehension to being jobless equals a fear of Caucasians. They will revel in people of color's reluctance to be poor, misinterpreting this as a fear or respect for the temporary authority whites hold in the office.

This is the root of the many mind games whites utilize as they toy with non-whites on the job.

The best way to thrive in this atmosphere is to enter the workplace and say to them and yourself, "I'm not here to play with white people."

Go on. Try it right now. Say it out loud.

"I'm not here to play with white people."

White people think you're here to entertain or play with them. And rest assured, they are definitely going to play with you. So, don't be surprised that you will never get that promotion if it's a non-white versus a white. Don't bet the bank on it. No matter how well you perform or what your credentials are.

## "PERFORMANCE REVIEW"

It's not you. It's not up to you. There is nothing you can do. Your work ethic on the job does not affect whites' decision or opinion of you.

It doesn't matter how hard you work to try to win over

whites' trust and show them that you are just like them. It's not that white people don't trust you. The truth is they don't intend to give you a chance to perform because you may excel and surpass them.

A steadfast rule to note when dealing with white people in the workplace is cowardice is professionalism.

Now, for best results with smaller issues on the job always try to get a face-to-face meeting. White people hate real communication. It makes them uncomfortable.

Tell them that your email is down. Don't take a call. Just show up at their cubicle or office. This showing up tactic is usually more effective with minor inconveniences like obtaining a report, letter, etc.

Remember, eighty percent of success is simply showing up.

## "PRIVATE EYES"

At any given time, if you look around, you'll see someone white staring at you, like you're on display. Like you're a specimen of some sort. Catch them looking and they'll avert their eyes. Or give you the fake smile.

In fact, sometimes you'll notice white people will smile at you for nothing and say "hello". This "speak and smile" tactic is the white way of saying, "Don't mind me. I'm harmless." But these are the most harmful whites.

Whenever a white person tries to relax you in the workplace, turn your defenses up. (If it's on the street, just pat yourself down and look for your wallet.) Everything a white person says to a person of color is the exact opposite of what they really mean.

In addition to simply staring at you like you are an exhibit at a museum, white people actually think it's their job to watch and monitor you as a citizen. They like to keep an eye on you just in case you do something that they think is inappropriate. This affords them the opportunity to be the first ones to call the police on you. They feel like they're the cops when there aren't any around.

## "A GOOD HUSTLE"

Stress kills.

Seriously.

For people of color's own health and survival, it is imperative that they alleviate any stimuli in their life that can attribute to stress. Like constantly swimming in a shark tank. Tickling a rattlesnake repeatedly. Crawling through a minefield on your way home. Or working with and for whites.

Anything that stresses you out will prove to be fatal over time. This is due to the unnaturally high levels of anxiety that you must maintain in order to endure the experience.

Therefore, when you absolutely must work with whites, view it as a temporary assignment, even if it has to be long term. Do it only until you can figure a way to get out and work for yourself or with other people of color.

For non-whites, working with and for Caucasians is like hustling in the street. Plan on only doing it temporarily. Attempt to position yourself where you don't have to work with and for them for an extended period of time.

Prolonged exposure to the games white people play in the workplace can be draining and cancerous. You'll sometimes find yourself interacting harshly with people outside of your workplace the same way that whites deal with you on the job.

This is a sign of the early stages of the poisoning. Having a job with whites should always be perceived as nothing more than a hustle. A temporary arrangement.

# CHAPTER FIVE
## POLICE

The police are here to protect and serve...

...rich, white people.

When a child reaches the age of eighteen or finishes high school they are expected to leave their parent's home.

Normally, those teens with proper preparation go on to college. Without college, some will find a job in a clerical position following high school.

For most, without the means to pursue further education, they are faced with two options: the military and the police academy.

Both organizations need bodies.

And they are always hiring.

The more adventurous and courageous young adults will select the military, while the lazy and cowardly select the police force.

In some rare occasions, a small percentage of these individuals enlist in either institution because they may have relatives that were soldiers or police officers. However, the majority of these individuals are faced with limited alternatives.

Since the police decision is the easiest to select between the two, it becomes the final choice for those who are forced to leave their parents' house and get a job.

So they become a cop.

Understanding this drive is fundamental as you consider the thought processes and actions of police.

Equally important is recognizing that the police system was created in order to control and terrorize ex-slaves and to also fight the unity of coal miners.

This is not a "for the people" organization.

It takes nothing to be a cop.

No special skills, no qualifications, nothing.

Cops are not required to have a thorough social educational background or a criminal justice degree.

Being a cop is not a service police perform out of the goodness of their hearts.

It's a paycheck.

They do it to get paid.

Getting paid requires good performance.

To be considered for good performance, a cop must make more arrests.

This foundation creates a natural, ongoing conflict of interest between people of color and police.

Every time a non-white interacts with a cop, the officer is endeavoring to arrest that person of color.

## "LOOSE LIPS SINK SHIPS"

Don't talk to police.

When interacting with police, remember that they are always, ALWAYS trying to figure out a way to arrest you.

Never talk to police.

Minimize interaction with them.

Occasionally, you may find yourself pulled over for a DNW (Driving Non-White) violation. The so-called "routine" traffic stop. The only thing routine about it is the consistent harassment that the police system has been known for.

In any event, if you find yourself stopped by a police officer, remember that you are smarter than a cop.

They settled on that job because they couldn't do anything else. Don't let them fool or trick you during this inconvenience.

The entire justice system is distorted from the roots, but some of these practices may work to your benefit some of the time when pulled over in your vehicle by police.

Never say you know why you are being stopped. You don't know anything.

Put your cell phone on the dashboard before the cop arrives at your window and record the conversation. Call someone. Call your voicemail. Use the voice memo feature. Be your own witness because police are trained to lie.

Go with the obvious, keep your hands in sight, and no sudden movements.

Hide your personal belongings because they can't search you unless you say so.

Although it might sound casual, if a cop asks is it okay if he searches your pockets, your reply should always be no. They ask because they can't do it without your consent.

You can't be searched without your permission. If you can't be searched, the cops can't plant anything either.

By law, you have the right to tell police you do not consent to any searches.

Remember, don't talk to police.

All you should have for police is, "No, you cannot search me or my vehicle", "Am I free to go?" and "I'll only speak with an attorney."

Other than that, don't talk to police.

You can't work out a deal with police. They are not on your side. They are not giving you a break.

The grim reality is that people of color's interactions with police just don't happen to be so cordial and courteous.

Still, try to not invite them to you. Give them no reason to pull you over.

Find an uncle, aunt, boyfriend, or girlfriend, and get the paperwork right on your car. Get that taillight fixed.

Traffic stops don't always go so routine. Cops believe they have some authority over you. The basis of their interaction with you is to humiliate you.

So, not only should people of color avoid and minimize their dealings with police, it serves non-whites' interest to begin to alter the systems that employ and empower such civil servants.

### "CHANGE THE GAME"

White people are afraid of people of color, so they support any police abuse, harassment, or brutality.

Even by silence.

The reason white people are sometimes more likely to be courageously rude to you is because they know that if or when the police arrive, the cops will protect them.

White people know that if anything goes to court, they are more likely to win versus a non-white.

The entire justice system needs an overhaul, from the judges to the politics and down to the cops.

It is all a western white system built on preserving corruption and injustice.

In the long term, it needs to be changed.

In the short term, people of color can create a shift in the abusive relations that they have with the cops simply by raising awareness at the unjust practices.

Police brutality and abuse perpetuates as a result of a variety of factors.

The freedom to do so, the way whites view non-whites, citizens unaware of their power, etc.

Police were never set up to be fair and protective, but now they fall under the cities' jurisdiction.

They are supposed to serve the people and the communities in the cities that they are employed.

Each city has a council. You can get involved. People of color can get their people involved.

Once you have a presence in the city council, steps can be taken from there to change the power that the beat cops have. From making sure the cops that are in your community are actually from your community to severe time and punishment for police murders, harassment, and abuse.

Ask an entertainer that you respect (singer, actor, rapper) to be on the city council for your neighborhood.

Don't believe it can be done?

The Terminator is the governor of California.

Your favorite entertainer wields tremendous influence. They can amass the votes. They can force abusive police out of your neighborhoods.

Don't view it as politics. View it as a means to fight the cops.

If the entertainer angle is too extreme, select someone you trust. Don't have anyone? Find someone. Craft your representative.

This is at the smallest level because most individuals interested in politics or being a councilperson are only interested in being a mayor, senator, or president. The further along one ventures in that tangled web, the more corruptible they are. Corrupt officials don't help fight police abuse.

This city council angle is but one method of dealing with police, but it's most important that people of color recognize that police are not their friends, allies, or protectors. From this standpoint, no matter the length of time, more solutions to dealing with police can be mapped out.

# CHAPTER SIX
## WHITE PEOPLE & ENTERTAINMENT

### "RUN THE WORLD"

With dominance, entertainment affairs influence the globe.

Ask anyone to name five politicians that have not been in the news in the last year. Now ask them to name their favorite singers, actors, or movies.

You may find yourself trapped in a week-long conversation.

It is important to realize that all of popular culture: news, books, magazines, music, TV, sports and movies are controlled by whites.

Jewish whites to be exact. Again, they run every single branch of popular culture.

They also control the representation of the talent and distribution of the content.

One group of people controlling all of popular opinions

creates a very natural conflict of interest for people of color.

Ask yourself, when have white people EVER had people of color's best interest in mind?

When?

The history of white people's relations with non-whites has been negative since the first time they arrived on everyone's shores. The records won't reflect them turning magically pleasant yesterday.

Or even tomorrow.

Does that mean you hate them?

No.

You adapt. There is more than enough history available on Caucasians, and now is the time to adapt to their behavior patterns.

Consider the following pipeline in one facet of entertainment: film and TV.

The channels a movie idea must pass through before it receives a "green light" for shooting travels from writer to agent to production company to network and then onto a studio.

The big six agencies (CAA, WMA, ICM, Endeavor, Paradigm, UTA) are all run by the same type of people: White Jewish People.

The production companies and networks are all run by the same type of people: White Jewish People.

The studios (Sony, Universal, Paramount, Fox, WB, Disney) are all run by the same type of guys that run the agencies, production companies, and networks.

White Jewish People.

There's no diversity.

Although product is marketed to every racial group, behind the scenes only one group of people are pulling the strings.

There's no diversity.

The same can be said about the distribution of information, the news, newspapers, etc.

These industries are run by the same guys who run the TV and movie studios. They see the world one way.

So, the news stories or TV shows and films that they run or "green light" will reflect the world through a Jewish lens.

There's no diversity.

Most people of color have little Jewish awareness because quite naturally all they are seeing is another white person.

And this is all that really matters. Not the labels.

Because, at this point, it is as simple as white people controlling the entertainment and information that people of color receive.

This is a problem.

At one point in time, white people thought they were the best basketball players.

Because they were the only ones playing.

This was before black people began to play.

Right now, whites think they are the only ones qualified to control information and entertainment for everyone. They figure they can and should decide what's suitable for everyone else.

When one group of people control the entertainment that is produced for everyone, then the product is going to be biased to that one group's views and opinions of what is acceptable for art and expression.

## "DESTROY THEIR ART"

You may notice that most successful people of color in entertainment today are completely silent when it comes to any social issues.

In the past, people of color in entertainment used their voices to help their people.

But, in order to play, you must be approved by whites.

At different points in time, people of color controlled their own stories, expression, and arts. Time and time again, whites would infiltrate, destroy, and attempt to master these arts.

Whenever a group of color encounters white people, whites begin a nonstop crusade to constantly cripple people of color by crippling their artistic expression.

Take America for instance. Examine black art through the

drum.

Music.

The drum is essential to all people of color from the lion dance in China to the step show at a Black university.

Systematically, whites have begun to weaken blacks through the destruction of black music in America.

Just as McDonald's targets children to ensure life-long customers, Caucasians play for keeps. For the long term.

Through their control of media and media outlets they can handpick black entertainers.

So, as they replace the voices that spoke of pride and cultural awareness over soulful instrumentation with newer voices that speak of murder and blatant materialism over computer noise, then they will in effect begin to change the mindset of black people.

Whites will use black entertainers to erode cultural pride, awareness, and social consciousness in blacks.

The irony of black entertainers or glam-rappers boasting about their so-called riches is that being black or being a person with color is synonymous with poverty.

You are as your people are.

In other words, each black person is a representative of their people. So, no matter how many diamonds a black entertainer may have on, when that entertainer's people are poor, the entertainer is poor.

Masked poverty is what the world sees when black entertainers elect to flaunt or make songs about white people's wealth, which is not true wealth. Real wealth is land and the means to protect your land.

It's interesting to note that centuries ago, the Trans-Atlantic Slave Trade was aided at certain points by blacks actually selling other blacks. Just as now, black entertainers continue to align with whites to sell poisonous entertainment to their own people.

The entertainers don't realize that a hypothetical spot in the big house when your people are slaves still makes the entertainer a slave.

Nothing that white people give non-whites is helpful.

Whether it's the check cashing/pawn shops, liquor stores, or soulless entertainment personalities.

People of color should reject it all.

White people's media outlets and the entertainment they approve serves to show blacks that they are on an auction block of sorts.

This deterioration and lack of respect for black music outlines the design for destroying a people through their art.

As whites push their version of what is acceptable entertainment to blacks, they will claim the true essence of black people's ethnic art and expression for themselves.

In recent times, the media indicates that the female soul singers are white women hailing from England. They've even crowned one of these singers "The New Queen of Soul". It is no coincidence that they are now reporting that a white guy is the king of rap music.

They destroy the people by destroying their culture. Then, they resurrect it with their own faces and images, and suddenly, it's "cool" again.

All the while, Caucasians will promote and endorse black entertainment that is subpar.

You will notice that whites love to hear the most negative and degrading songs from blacks. Songs that perpetuate the stereotypes that Caucasians created.

As the people's art and music die, so will the people. For they will lose their connection with themselves as they are severed from their own culture and history.

When the destruction of the art process begins to take shape within any group of non-whites, they should firmly halt the involvement of white people in their arts and affairs.

Otherwise, whites will destroy and steal your art, then replace you with themselves to bolster their image in the world view.

## "IMAGE IS EVERYTHING"

White people like to see white people.

They like whites.

This is why their image is plastered everywhere with zero to little diversity. On billboards, posters, advertisements, etc.

This is why there are not as many non-white stories in the entertainment that they control and view.

They are obsessed with convincing the world that they are great. White people flood the media with an onslaught of images of themselves as happy, in charge, strong, fair, and just, while depicting non-whites as angry, bumbling, and foolish.

Caucasians create larger than life white superheroes and ultra-stylized action and glamour icons. These "super" images serve to perpetuate white worship and to cripple non-white's esteem and compensate for the true inadequacies that Caucasians suffer from.

The more someone focuses on telling you that they are superior, the higher the probability that they are not.

If the "white is might" message were true, then it wouldn't need a constant, lifelong advertising campaign or reminder. It would be self-evident.

It's like a hyena scrambling around the jungle proclaiming to be king. The lion would never do that. The world knows its greatness.

At the decision-making level, white marketing and media executives will comment, "Well, this is what the people wanna see".

So, this indicates that in addition to the whites that control the information, the general white public also does not care for diversity. People of color must recognize and accept this reality.

Why is it important for whites to make it appear that people of color are always in conflict, fighting amongst each other, and can only be saved, rescued, or civilized by whites?

What are the long-term effects of always portraying darker people as aggressive and enraged, while whites are smiling?

As far as film and TV, if you see these images repeatedly-- especially the more blatant ones--it will take a toll on your sense of self and your people.

If you peel back the layers in entertainment and media, you will notice that they portray the darker people as combative, warrior types.

What this does is plant a seed in non-white people that makes them think of themselves as a threat to society.

A problem.

Not powerful, but chaotic.

Especially sports figures. They are always portrayed as mindless, animalistic brutes. Photographs are always printed with them yelling, never smiling.

To turn the tables on this bigotry, people of color should segregate themselves completely in sports.

For instance, in football, what if one team had all white running backs, wide receivers, quarterbacks, offensive and defensive lineman?

How would whites like it if all the white players played on one team and all the black players played on another?

Same for basketball and other sports.

How would superiority be viewed then?

A small change like this would cause the media to show more respect to the non-white athletes.

At the present, whites in power will make themselves and their people appear favored at all costs. In addition, when people of color look bad, white people shine.

In white societies that are ruled by sport and entertainment, the destruction, mockery, and ridicule of dominant non-white figures is of the utmost importance.

The Caucasian philosophy sees all other cultures separate, disconnected and inferior to them. To strengthen and validate that thinking, people of color are rarely given chances to show intelligence in white-run entertainment.

Any efforts or attempts are stifled.

Asking white people to view non-white people in a positive way is a moot point.

As people of color begin to cease asking whites to depict them respectfully, they will begin to entertain themselves.

Since the popular music that non-whites hear and view are all controlled by Caucasians, trustworthy people of color must create and run new talent agencies, production companies, music distributors, networks, and studios that are separate and free from White control or influence

Through the newly established media outlets, useful, honest information as well as empowering images of people of color must be programmed.

Negative images and perception can become a dangerous reality. It is mandatory that non-whites seize control of the depiction of their likenesses.

Being entertained and informed by those who have done you harm is detrimental to yourself and race.

Whites will also uphold the modern portrayed image of themselves and expect stereotypes from non-whites in day-to-day encounters.

# CHAPTER SEVEN
## WHITE & NON-WHITE GENDER RELATIONS

Men or women of color will find their interactions with whites of the opposite sex more tense, hostile, and confrontational.

There are many varying reasons why and several methods of adapting favorably in these situations.

### "DAMSEL IN DISTRESS"

In popular white stories, films, and TV shows, you may count one token male of color amongst a cast of white males. The non-white male may sometimes be paired with a white female.

Or, the white female character may also play the role of consoling the male of color when the white males mistreat him.

Over time, ideas like these convey the message that men of

color are either equal to or lesser than a white woman.

For white women, this portrayal reinforces existing racist outlooks, carrying over into their day-to-day interactions.

White women will engage non-white males of color according to the stereotype or idea that whites want to reduce them to.

For instance,

- Latinos - Workers
- Blacks - Dumb, sex machines
- Asians & East Indians - Cute, cuddly pets

It's up to the men to destroy these and many other negative perceptions of their people and culture.

Whether the men of color detect the subtle disrespect or present themselves in an intelligent manner, white women will always be more likely to be more confrontational with them as opposed to a woman of color.

This is because white females know tension or conflict won't resolve with a fight with the man of color. They will antagonize the non-white men, but not the women.

The white woman is quicker to engage or amplify an issue with a non-white male because they know a man shouldn't hit or fight her.

Also, conflict with a non-white male affords the white woman an opportunity to cry out to the white male for help.

The white woman loves to falsify and exaggerate her danger in order to be rescued. And, the white male cannot wait to come running. He knows how perverted his history is and he would hate for white women to endure the same crimes that he committed against women of color.

Don't feed a white woman's ego. Crush it.

If you pass one on the street, hold your nose. Pretend you've smelled something foul. Be creative.

If men of color pursue white women, worshipping them like the larger than life images that are projected, this will lead to further complications and lack of respect amongst the races.

If anything, let her pursue you. But, to save aggravation, men of color would fare better eliminating unnecessary dealings with them.

When dealing with a feisty white woman, black and Latino men have the option of alerting a woman from their respective cultures to deal with the white woman directly.

White women will never assault a black or Latino woman with a verbal barrage the way they would a man of color. They know a few disrespectful exchanges will escalate into a fistfight.

Asian and East Indian men, however, must be more firm when encountering a confrontational white woman. White women don't fear Asian and East Indian women the same way that they fear black and Latino women. So it's more beneficial for these males of color to never present themselves in a docile way when interacting with white females.

## "TO CATCH A PREDATOR"

Just as white women are prone to be more aggressive with males of color, the courage of white males will surge when interacting with non-white women.

Gestures, words, and actions that they would never use with a non-white man become the norm when dealing with women of color.

If a white male interacts with a woman of color in the absence of a non-white male, the Caucasian male is liable to try to intimidate or insult the non-white female.

In other circumstances, he will always overstep his boundaries and try to steer a conversation in a sexual direction.

When women of color are in public without a male of color and they experience or sense disrespect from a white male, they should try to spot a male of their color and ask a random question. Once the white man notes the presence of another male of color, he will scatter or interact with a non-white female more respectfully.

When dealing with white males, women of color should command the utmost respect at all times. Any disrespect allowed will be exploited to no end. Whites won't stop themselves; you have to.

If women of color find themselves violated or disrespected by a white male and there are no men of color around, come back with one. Always. Let the men of color catch the predator.

Non-whites often find themselves interacting with "nice", older, white men. White men, who in old age, suddenly want to be polite and cordial. People of color should never forget that what they are seeing when they come across an old white person is a lifetime of racism.

How many slurs do you think he has uttered in his life? Remember, no race of men on the planet has a more perverse past filled with the rape of women from other cultures than white males.

In the Americas, the Latinas from Mexico and Puerto Rico and everywhere else that white men arrived were raped. The modern descendants stand as evidence that the entire race was tainted by whites.

The same can be said for the black women who arrived here as slaves. The modern blacks in America today all show traces of slave owners' predatory, sexual violations. Very few blacks in America retain 100% African features.

To this day, some women of color can never relax around a white male.

Considering the white male's past, this comes as no surprise.

It's beneficial to remember that whites will never tell you their history or offer you anything allowing you to truly help yourself.

# CHAPTER EIGHT
## THE MASK

Racism at its core is an issue that has not been fully and honestly examined or discussed. Therefore, it is impossible for it to go away.

Whites won't expose anything.

Everything in this book, white people already know.  But, they will pretend not to.

## "WELL AWARE"

White people know what they are capable of. They know the innate hatred that resides in them. Hatred that's been stoked for millennia from living in the cold and running from disease.

They know. They know their makeup.

They have no faith in themselves because they know what they are comprised of.

It is the people of color who sometimes need convincing. In some cases, they have more faith in whites than whites have in themselves. Whites will not break this faith and share the truth about their nature.

Consider this: skin bleaching is at an all-time high around the globe.

Do not wait for whites to make an attempt at stopping the growth of the "worship-white" seeds that they planted.

They will not.

White people are all too mindful of their crimes and the negative effect that their contact has had on non-whites. They will don a disguise of friendship and well wishes, but will never share with people of color the true nature of their actions.

Since whites arm themselves with information as their primary weapon, that means on average, some whites know more about people of color's history than people of color actually do.

Whites know how racist they are and they know exactly what their people did to the world.

Remember that whites went so far as to beat white love and worship into entire cultures.

Beaten…as in by aggressive, violent force.

Whites won't drop their mask and tell you this. And they won't help you to drop the habits of adoring them and hating yourself.

It is up to people of color to share the stories with their youth and babies so that they will never make the mistake of trusting whites again.

Caucasians know the full extent of the damage their people have inflicted on the world, even when they pretend not to understand the conditions non-whites currently live in.

There would be no plight for some people of color had they never came in contact with whites in the first place.

Be cautious of white people pretending to clean up a mess they created only so they can be lauded as saviors.  This does not mean that they are helping you. Direct contact with them and their systems and customs has done more harm than good for people of color.

Their politics, banking, interest, credit, and school systems have not fared well for non-whites.

Expect whites to pretend not to know this and to adopt an indifferent and naive position when asked directly. Suddenly, they will seem to not know history.

### "WHITE PEOPLE B.S. DECODER"

As people of color begin to take note of the dishonest nature of whites, they will begin to employ a natural B.S. Decoder to translate what Caucasians say and do.

A few examples:

- Whites say: "Let the past go."

  Decoded: "Let us do what we want and shut up"

- Whites say: "Thank you for your help."

  Decoded: "Screw you. You're still a slave."

- Whites say (re: a racist outburst): "I lost the control."

  Decoded: "I let the mask slip off and lost my disguise."

- Whites say: "The indigenous natives are savage."

  Decoded: "I'll accuse you of being what I am."

Whites know their nature and their deeds. People of color should not wait until white people experience a racist meltdown to begin accepting them for what they are.

## "LET IT SLIP"

Encourage white people to let the mask slip all the way off. Stop acting surprised.

Asking whites not to be racist bigots puts a tremendous amount of pressure on them. Don't force their hands. Let them be themselves. Try to see their true skin.

Let them make little racists comments. Anticipate this and much, much, much worse. And, when they "slip up", just nod and make a mental note to self.

Don't push to ban their expression. Let them march. Let them assemble. Then observe them.

Honesty is the best policy.

It's important to let whites be themselves just as non-whites must be true to their culture. Be honest with white people and force them to show you their real colors.

Non-whites need to see Caucasians in their purest forms so they can realize what they are up against.

Let the mask slip all the way off. Let them reveal themselves.

Remember that whites will kill babies and children to reach their enemies, and then accuse their enemies of using the children as a shield. So which is worse? Using a child as a shield or shooting and murdering one?

Injustice at the hands of whites knows no bounds. It does not matter if you are an adult, child, rich or poor. Know this and see Caucasians without the mask of innocence.

People of color must know and readily identify those who have always done their people harm. And they must not forget. It doesn't matter if whites allow you to get a job with them. Or if they give you a record deal. Or put your favorite actor in one of their movies. Or if they give you a three-hundred dollar stimulus check. It does not change their nature.

People of color will begin to reevaluate the way they

interact with white people as they realize that it's the whites against the rest of the world. Against all of the non-white people. The animals. The elements. Earth, air, and water. Whites have polluted them all.

Up to this point, the method with which people of color have dealt with whites has not worked out for them. Non-white people would be wise to let the mask slip all the way off of whites so that the threat and danger that Caucasians pose can be clearly assessed.

# CHAPTER NINE
## THE TRAP

People of color should never stop demanding respect and justice. To this day, people in Hawaii are still protesting to win back their independence and combat white imperialism. However, dealing with white people is rarely a straightforward affair.

Caucasians set complex traps, and like the many treaties they have broken, their customs and ways are laden with deception. Be mindful and leery of the following deceptive sayings and practices.

### "WE'RE ALL A LITTLE BIT RACIST"

It starts off like this:  A white person will do or say something racially insensitive or offensive. The person of color may be hesitant or too shocked to address the offense. It's important to follow one's instincts. If you feel that it's racism, then it usually is.

So, once you call the white person on the racist act, they try to get you to prove it or to clearly articulate it just to see if you fully picked up on it.

Then they will joke, "We're all a little bit racist" and try to coerce you into poking fun at another culture's differences.

First things first. All people cannot be racist. In order to be racist, your race must have a position of power and control throughout the world. Only whites fit this description.

Second, the idea of racism has always been skewed to benefit the white, white-like, or light people. It has never been about darker people oppressing the light or white people. People of color just don't have that same history as whites. Once Caucasians left Western Europe, the world began negative change for all people of color.

Third, a person of color should never follow whites and join them with racist jokes.

If you are not white, and your people have come in contact with Caucasians, you have experienced the same injustice.

Racist jokes aimed at people of color are about as tasteful as "your mother..." jokes when someone's mother has recently died.

There is nothing funny.

Whites want to drag you into being barbaric by making you think you and your people are just as blameful as theirs. This is clearly not the case.

## "AUTOPILOT"

People of color should be careful if they remove themselves from direct contact with whites only to continue to implement Caucasian practices. Falling into this trap can have the same effects as dealing with whites firsthand.

Occasionally, whites will throw a docile person of color at the head of an organization or business where the employees are mostly white. This does not mean the company is run by a person of color.

White people can invade and occupy your country, leave, yet still remain there in practice.

When people of color evict Caucasians from their lands, it's equally important that they eliminate the systems, businesses, and practices of whites.

Because the trap is the effects of what whites leave behind, you can endure "white people hell" without them being around.

The poverty. Self-hate. Tension. Conflict. Despair. Stress over money. These thought processes that may have been initially inflicted upon non-whites to cripple them can continue to run indefinitely without whites at the wheel.

## "MAKE SOME MONEY"

Whites place high importance on money because they are the only ones who have it. It gives them an unfair advantage. Unfortunately, however, the primary language in the world is not English or Mandarin, but money.

If white people have all of the money, how are you ever going to catch them? It's a losing battle.

They've made money more important than anything. They created that paradigm. So, slowly try to free yourself from pursuing their money.

Real wealth is not money, however. Real wealth is land.

Not their money.

If financial systems crash and you had several bank accounts with large sums of money in them, what good does that do you?

But what if you own several farms?

That's real wealth.

When people of color think they cannot survive without whites' money and monetary systems, then they have fallen into one of the greatest traps.

Non-whites should not let financial woes terrorize them into accepting something even worse than slavery.

There are ten-year-old children in India that hand stitch soccer balls for a nickel an hour to pay off lifelong debts that they incurred buying medicine.

This should never happen.

White people's money is the most dangerous pitfall that persons of color could ever fall into.

The fear of not having any money. Losing money. If Caucasian's economic systems fall or crash, don't lose your wits. Your wits can't be taken away from you.

Also maintain good health. Health is true wealth. Whites know this. That is why the land and countries that white people have interest in suddenly become disease filled. Health is wealth. Not white people's money.

Don't let the things that they make important to them take precedence in your life.

Money is just a piece of paper.

It's not land, grass, trees, fertile soil. It's not livestock, mountain springs, lumber, or even bronze.

It is unnatural to give control to something that cannot sustain you naturally.

Money is not trout, whiting, or salmon.

Money and monetary systems are little of pieces of paper, averages, and digital tickers.

Money is not real. Grain is. Wheat is. Apple juice is.

Don't let the financial woes make you lose your marbles. The planet earth will sustain you.

Current financial systems and models are established by

whites who generally have an adverse history with people of color. It can be increasingly difficult to win at a game created by those who have done you harm.

A game that is set up for whites to win and for you to lose. A game that, if and when you decide to play, you will always be far behind them.

Such is the game of economic success or the attainment of their wealth.

The faster non-whites run on that carrot wheel, the quicker they will tire themselves out. In the process, losing the interest and energy needed to strengthen their minds.

People of color have been born with means to sustain themselves naturally from the land...without a bank account or a credit card.

This is why the school and office setting systems don't truly resonate with non-whites. Because people of color are a people of nature, and being cooped up inside a Caucasian's building doing something that does not exercise you physically is not natural.

Harmony with nature means reaping what you sow and being naturally equipped to provide just enough for yourself and your family. Not exploiting the earth's resources as gluttonous whites continue to do on a day-to-day basis.

People of color will begin to experience true wealth once

they move away from the synthetic customs and systems that harm them and move forward toward their original nature.

## "LESSER EVILS"

A large misconception that non-whites have is that they are obligated to select from the choices that Caucasians set before them.

People of color are no longer required to choose from the options that whites leave behind. The time is now for non-whites to create their own options.

Take a very simple conversation example: A person of color decides to make a stand for his or her own cultural group. Whites will attack them, and in conversation, ask something unrelated like, "So you want to kill all whites?" or "Do you hate white people?"

But, that person of color can reply by saying that they reject both suggestions and go on to clearly communicate their position.

Or, a large instance: Choosing between two rich, white candidates to govern poor people. This is illogical. Non-white people are beginning to learn the advantages of crafting their own options established by themselves and for their own benefit.

## "SHADOW BOXING"

No matter what, people of color should always acknowledge and say hello to their fellow people of color in passing. Always.

Over time, whites have encouraged the process of white love and ethnic hate, especially amongst non-whites. Caucasians will incite people of color to fight themselves based on information that whites provide. This is the white way of working through people of color by having them hate what white people hate.

People of color should never fall for the trap of going against other cultures because white people told them to. White people will instigate and have poor people fighting one another, thinking their cousins, brothers, and sisters are their enemies.

Also, with a full knowledge of history and its effects, white people will accuse other cultures of similar crimes knowing that these non-whites are clashing over white money, jobs, and interests. This deception and feigned ignorance is a crime unto itself.

Don't let white people tell you that another person of color is the blame for your poverty the way that they pit Zimbabweans against South Africans in Africa or Blacks against Mexicans for white people's jobs.

The truth of the matter is it's white people versus the rest of the world. End of story. Check history. They have screwed everyone and everything over equally.

If you have whites in your land, chances are times are hard for the people of color, but everything is fine for the whites.

The whites are going to deflect attention away from themselves by telling you that another non-white culture is the problem, encouraging dissension and tension among non-whites so they can never unify.

People of color should be careful of fighting themselves. Energy should be focused on fighting against and gang-banging on the white systems that can ruin them.

The true fight for non-whites is not a physical fight with people of color, but a mental one with white people's paradigms.

Combat this. Focus all of your anger and animosity on that.

All unchecked aggression should be rechanneled from physical aggression into mental aggression.

Then aim your intelligence at your real enemies: the systems that whites have in place. The media, schooling, financial constructs, etc.

Train your anger on these real enemies and figure out a way to combat, attack, and riot against those systems.


## "CHASING WHITE"

The first law of nature is self-preservation.

Not chase white people.

It's imperative that people of color stop attempting to find a crack in whites' program to permanently insert themselves in.

Non-whites will fare much better to pursue the preservation of their people regardless of cues from whites.

Early on, the desire for equality became confused and purposely misinterpreted as a need for acceptance into the white world.

Success was associated with being white. Money meant white. People of color set out to fight economic hardship, and in some cases, they found themselves always at the coattails of whites.

People of color should realize what true wealth is. It is not being white or having white money. In fact, no action or motives of non-whites should be predicated by a negative or positive stimulus from white people.

People of color's actions should be executed with the goal of preserving themselves and a future for their offspring.

The old ways were if whites were polite, then you respond nicely. Or if whites call you a slur, then you get angry.

This is too much control over the cultures.

Following the cues of whites can leave you at a disadvantage because they can and will misdirect you.

Break this control and focus on preservation with or without whites and regardless of what whites do to you. Whether they are malicious or polite. Whether they hire or fire you.

Temporarily working with whites is only a means and not the end.

Remember that you do not simply want the company of whites. You want a balanced, healthy means of sustenance, which may not even require their financial ideas, systems, and worthless paper money with their faces on it.

Don't just aspire to work in their building. Leave their building and create a new alternate method of commerce.

Running a race on a track that whites built surely spells defeat for people of color. When people don't intend to be poor, they should focus on that and what it will require to truly escape poverty. Not simply trying to be white or having what whites have.

When you follow behind whites, you will always be just that--behind them.

# CHAPTER TEN
## "I WISH I WERE WHITE" PEOPLE

Occasionally, encounters will arise with persons of color who seem more intent upon furthering the interests or customs of whites.

Everything that has been discussed in this book with reference to whites should be magnified by four or five when dealing with non-whites who love Caucasians more than themselves. "I wish I were white" people need to be dealt with just as cautiously as whites, or even more so at times.

Because they will try harder.

Any injustice or rudeness expected by whites will be intensified at the hands of those who wish they were white but are not. Their struggle is born out of the unique circumstance which forces them to prove their "whiteness" to themselves and to whites.

That's double the convincing. Double the effort.

Consider that in Asia, as a result of white interests and influence, the Japanese neglect to even illustrate Asians in their animation and video games. They use their talents to draw white people to tell their own stories.

Even in the U.S., as whites clearly communicate who is considered an "American" by skewing their laws and policies to favor whites or prominently displaying whites on the majority of their magazine covers and billboards in every city, non-whites still clamor to be included and referred to as American.

This tell-one-thing-and-show-another tactic affects people of color by intensifying Caucasian worship.

As a result, some ethnic groups fashion or formulate an unnatural hatred for people of color by adopting the hatred of what whites despise most: non-white people.

In some cases, where one person of color intends to fully integrate into the white world, they may go so far as to shed their own ethnicity and hate the current culture that whites are mocking at the time.

For example, when Asians hate blacks or when East Indians hate Latinos, they are completely oblivious to the asinine nature of feigning racism against someone with the same complexion as them.

Black and Latino cops are notorious for this cowardice.

When they join the racist police force, the unspoken rule is that they must choose the color that is neither black nor brown, but blue, consequently turning a blind eye and deaf ear to brutality, abuse, and murder of their own people.

Whites create the catalyst for this behavior through their rejection of difference.

Even when Caucasians do something minor like flinching when they hear a voice deeper than their own, this causes some non-whites to make their voices squeaky in order to be accepted as "talking white".

Practices like these on a small and large scale serve to condition some individuals of color, forcing them to assimilate and become something other than what they are naturally.

### "ACTING WHITE"

White people came, saw, and told the people who welcomed them that they were inferior.

This was a key component in the erection of the colonies that whites set up in lands that were not theirs.

Whites left these colonies after establishing control of the resources, the indigenous people's minds, or by force. In some countries like South Africa, whites remain and haven't been forced out yet.

Upon the withdrawal of the whites, some people of color

began to assume the identities and the customs of their prior colonists. These are the early roots of non-whites mimicking the behavior of Caucasians.

Over time, those who elected to follow behind the white colonists had to accept what the whites would hate, even if it meant hating themselves.

This allows racism to exist in a place like India where Caucasian colonization is a thing of the past, but the ideas of the white colonists can cause the lighter persons to mistreat the darker.

The world over, Caucasians told the people of color that they were primitive, outdated, and uneducated.

Naturally, as non-whites begin to don formal western-styled schooling and dress, they were accused of "acting white".

"Acting white" is not simply reduced to being western schooled. It also extends to mannerisms that people of color may pick up from white people, such as raising the pitch of their voice unnecessarily, pretending that your body temperature is cold, or like you are afraid of everything and everyone, and the shedding of or complete ignorance of your own culture.

The irony of people of color doing their best white people impersonation is that the entire masquerade is performed to be approved by whites, but whites don't have the final say and authority of cultural approval.

No one does.

Furthermore, regardless of the impersonation, whites still won't "approve" of the non-white individual. They will only lose more respect for the non-white as these actions force the person of color into a more subservient position.

And whites will always abuse authority.

Being educated or knowledgeable never meant being white. In fact, western, white, formal schooling alone is not enough to make a person completely educated or knowledgeable.

Being well groomed, spoken, or respectful is not a characteristic of being white. Chances are if you are a person of color, your people have inhabited the planet earth long before whites. In each culture, there is ceremonial, proper dress and there are well spoken poets and writers.

Whites visited every nation inhabited by people of color and gave the people new identities.

Caucasians will steal non-white's culture and identity then repackage it and claim it for themselves.

Civilization is synonymous with people of color. They should not associate polite traits or being educated with white people.

Non-white cultures have their own practices, education, and measures of intelligence. It is not mandatory that they be Caucasian based or Euro-centric.

People of color should seize Caucasian's schooling, but always blend it with a deep understanding and appreciation of their own culture and history. Otherwise, they will run the risk of leading a life performing their best white people impression reaping no real benefits.

## "WHITE MAN'S BURDEN"

The White Man's Burden - a compelling pressure that forces whites to try to make everyone like them - has been carried out against people of color throughout the world.

In some non-whites, exposure to this stimulus has caused a poorly mistaken undying want for acceptance into white society.

Others maintain an indifferent position remarking, "Oh, it's okay. That's just the way things are."

The process can be reversed, however. It must be reversed for the survival of non-whites.

Consider, for example, that African and Asian leaders in their home countries shed their own culture's clothing and styles of dress for European attire. Although minor, this acceptance of whites' values over one's own contributes to a subconscious, dangerous worship of whites.

Why not create a modernized Kimono (Japan)?

There is nothing stopping people of color from updating the

designs of the clothing from their corresponding cultures. As non-white people open their minds, options will present themselves.

Don't let whites set the only standards of fashion, education, etc.

Women of color, there is no need for you to continue showering white women with praise like they are the only standard of beauty.

They will only tell you thank you.

They will never tell you that you are beautiful or encourage you to be yourself.

White people do not genuinely respect people of color's cultures or natural beauty.

When non-whites carry on the standards, ideas, and customs that Caucasians introduce them to, they run the risk of not only aspiring to be whatever they think white is, but they also risk becoming a racist in the process. This is what is meant by the racism without whites. But, it does not mean that racism is innate to all people.

Be mindful that you don't let white people's wants, desires, and opinions become your own over the long term or on a deep, mental level. Don't perpetuate the white man's burden for him in his absence.

# CHAPTER ELEVEN
## PRE-RESPONSE TO CRITICS

This book ain't for you.

It's for women of color who find themselves harassed by white police.

It's for men of color who are sick of being greeted with fearful stares from whites.

It's for children of color who hoped we were in a "post-racial" era only to find themselves kicked out of a public pool.

It's for little girls of color that have to go through the supermarket checkout aisles and see twenty magazine covers of blonde-haired white women and no women that look like themselves.

This is for all the people of color that don't see people that look like themselves on the billboards in their city.

There is no silent complacency.

If a people see themselves excluded from everything and ridiculed at every juncture, what are they supposed to be?

Happy?

Thrilled?

Overjoyed to see the images of everyone but themselves plastered in every media outlet throughout the world?

What do you expect a person of color to think?

They travel around a city and see images of whites and none of themselves. Is this supposed to make them pleasant? Or does logic dictate that tension would easily arise?

The entire planet has had an unpleasant relationship with white people. This is a problem that must be identified and addressed, or it will never go away.

It serves people of color's absolute best interest to start having these dialogues about white people. Then, real issues can make their way out into the open.

Whites have shown people of color their position, and now people of color are able to tell the world how they really feel.

Examine the small expanse of land of Western Europe. Why are the non-white people of the world all following the dress code, customs, and traditions of these lands?

The time is now for people of color to start asking these natural, understandable, logical, and rational questions.

Are truth, honesty, and the exposure of current state of

affairs for race relations offensive or derogatory?

Can you be supported by white folks and really be for the good of people of color? Is there any record of this in history?

Time and time again, when someone speaks truth and shines bright light on a racial issue, white people drag that person through the mud. Or murder them.

This sends a strong message to people of color from whites that essentially say, "Don't speak out against us."

Non-whites can't expect Caucasians to support their own exposure.

They have never been huge fans of truth.

Religious lies = white people

Political lies = white people

Educational lies = white people

Entertainment lies = white people

The time is now for these concerns to be discussed. When people of color have spoken out against racial injustice in the past, white people rush to accuse them of hating whites.

This couldn't be further from the truth.

In fact, it is irrelevant.

It is the non-whites' own concern with their survival that forces them to speak so sincerely.

It is not hate. In fact, it's love.

Love for their babies.

Love for their brothers, sisters, and cousins.

The kind of love that forces you to speak straight without sugarcoating.

When whites accuse a person of color who has stood up against injustices at the hands of whites as being "anti-white", an interesting train of thought arises.

If that person of color is fighting against lies, exploitation, and injustice, and whites are against that, then it would seem that white people are saying their way of life is one of oppression, dishonesty, and that it should be understood and accepted.

More importantly, by accusing someone that fights racial injustice as being anti-white, it mars that person's message, especially when it is a message of unity.

Dealing with the white oppressors is but one step.

Not the focal point.

The underlying messages are pro-color, pro-justice, pro-freedom, and pro-equality.

Not anti-white.

Some critics remark that, "Racism and race relations need time to heal" or "White people need time to learn how to respect others."

And people of color are supposed to wait? No.

White people don't delay their racist bigotry.

If white people want people of color's land, they don't delay.

If a white person grows tired of looking at a non-white face around the office, they don't say, "I'm sick of you, but in ten years we're going to fire you."

No. That person is fired immediately.

People of color must delay no longer in examining and understanding the nature and motives of white people. This book is to encourage people of color to share their experiences with these issues amongst each other so that they may know that they are not alone.

It is so that they can foster communication with one another, realizing that they are all facing the same issues, and together they can change the way they interact with white people.

This book is to help people of color share their experiences and inform them that they must be swift to educate themselves and their children. At this stage, there is little need for non-whites to be concerned with hating white people.

But, if people of color find themselves accused of such, they need only to inform their accusers that they don't hate white people.

It's just that they love people of color.

# CHAPTER TWELVE
## "COOL" WHITE PEOPLE

Very rare occasions will arise where people of color will encounter Caucasians with genuinely good and well-meaning intentions.

This is important to consider so that people of color won't let the adverse affects of negative race relations drive them insane. It's more beneficial to be aware and cautious, but not on edge.

Bearing that in mind, there have been sprinkles of isolated incidents where some whites have attempted to aid people of color in their plight, although whites may have been the cause of the plight in the first place.

Nevertheless, there were a handful of whites who fought apartheid. There are civil war letters written by white soldiers expressing their grief and dedication to fight against their own blood brothers for the rights of slaves.

You even have whites that have been assassinated by other whites when they stood up for racial justice.

These anomalies in Caucasians do exist. However, these types of whites are the minority. The exceptions. Not the steadfast, safe rule. These types of whites don't represent the whole of white people.

Suppose that three out of ten whites are genuinely humane, fair, and pleasant. That would leave seventy percent of whites that are malicious, prejudiced bigots. Hardly something to be ignored.

Thus, the mass generalizations are justified in order for people of color to protect themselves from harm or injustice at the hands of whites in the future.

## "I HAVE NON-WHITE FRIENDS"

"My best friends are Latino."

"My wife is Asian."

"Some of my best friends are black."

I am your friend. I am your friend.

I am not racist.

I am not racist.

These are common defenses whites will use in an effort to prove that they are not racist against people of color.

If non-whites intend to truly find out if Caucasians are their friends, they need only to bring up one man: O.J. Simpson.

Ask a white person that may seem "cool" what their thoughts are on the O.J. verdict, and they will quickly unmask their racism, while simultaneously revealing what they truly feel about their non-white "friends".

When whites rush to proclaim how many friends they have that are people of color, what they are really saying is, "I have non-white friends that wish they were white."

Just as in all of their systems and programs, whites will handpick the most docile and subservient people of color to round out their roster of "friends".

People of color should note that these whites do not generally have a respect for their cultures. This "friends" proclamation is nothing more than a dishonest charade that is part of them wearing the mask.

These whites are nothing like Caucasians that have used their influence and voice to expose other whites for injustice and unfair practices.

Even with those cases considered, however, in the exchanges people of color have had with white people, the bad still outweighs the good.

Non-whites shouldn't be in such a rush to hold hands and be friends with whites. If Caucasians were at the receiving end of the same abuse that they inflicted upon non-whites, Caucasians wouldn't be as forgiving as people of color.

White people will exploit non-whites' desire for friendship by telling them now "what's done is done" and forget about the past. As if persons of color should not object to the current state of race relations or poverty. It would seem that whites want non-whites to celebrate white people's success, be happy because white people are doing well, and disregard their own people's condition and status.

People of color must never forget that, overall, despite those rare occasions, white people do not defend them the way that they defend whites.

More often than not, white people's actions are always with disingenuous intentions. For instance, consider when whites make publicity trips to countries where the people are of color.

White people are not traveling to any country or community that they destroyed and readily admitting their faults and directly correcting them. This is never going to happen.

It is left to non-whites to identify the imbalanced relationship that they have with whites, work to strengthen the bonds with their own people, and rebuild their lands independent of Caucasian influence.

## "FROM HERE ON OUT"

People of color should see whites' true intentions when they offer "help" in their communities and lands. It is dangerous to think of these whites as friends.

Always keep their history in mind.

Occasionally, some whites remark that whites don't have an all encompassing monolithic plan or thought process.

Then people of color will notice that globally, Caucasians who have never met each other engage people of color with the exact same disrespect and injustice.

This proves that the disdain whites have for people of color is natural to Caucasians. People of color should never drop their defenses again and think that any whites have their best interest in mind.

If whites had natural respect, justice, and goodwill in their hearts for all humans, why is their history bloody everywhere that they traveled? Why don't they have a pleasant track record?

If whites were good-natured, why didn't they naturally respond peacefully and fairly to all of the people and lands they were welcomed to?

The evil that whites exhibited throughout history lies dormant in every one of them, like a wild animal sedated to perform a temporary stage show.

On a general, safe scale, there is no such thing as "cool" white people. But, if people of color continue to believe that such a thing exists, they will hurt themselves just as much as whites harm them from day to day.

This reveals the fundamental flaw that people of color have: they love.

They cannot hate to the core. People of color hope there is some good in others. They could never in a million years fathom the depths of what white people would plan for non-whites.

But, they must begin to.

People of color must try to imagine what acts white people would commit to preserve themselves.

It's much better to be safe than to be sorry and surprised.

History does not forecast a change in the relationships between people of color and whites.

For their survival and future, people of color absolutely must change the way they interact with whites.

However, ultimately, the best way to deal with white people is not to deal with them at all…in every aspect.

CPSIA information can be obtained at www.ICGtesting.com
Printed in the USA
BVOW070647150513

320755BV00002B/351/P